BC 39032

792.8   Sorine, Daniel S. and
SOR   Dancershoes

DATE DUE			
~~STAFF~~ ~~APR~~ ~~NOV 21 199~~			
NOV 21	JAN 0 2 2007		
~~FEB 7~~ ~~OCT 28~~			
~~JAN 3~~			
~~DEC 14~~			
JAN 22			

Dancershoes

Daniel S. Sorine &
Stephanie Riva
Sorine

Alfred A. Knopf
New York
1979

In memory of Savely Sorine and Boris Chaliapin

We thank the people who have guided and influenced our lives with the kind of inspiration that engenders zeal:
our mothers, Shirley Bassoff Silverman and Anna Sorine Chervachidze, and Mr. Philip Lynne.
We especially thank Martha Kaplan, Ellen McNeilly, Robert Scudellari, Sara Eisenman, Gennady Smakov,
and Marco Petrasese, and a devoted thank you to our editor, Robert Gottlieb.
We send all the dancers in this book kisses of appreciation, and wishes for continuing
beauty, health, and happiness.   *—Stephanie and Daniel Sorine*

THIS IS A BORZOI BOOK PUBLISHED BY ALFRED A. KNOPF, INC.

Copyright © 1979 by Stephanie Riva Sorine and Daniel S. Sorine.
All rights reserved under International and Pan-American Copyright Conventions. Published in the
United States by Alfred A. Knopf, Inc., New York, and simultaneously in Canada by
Random House of Canada Limited, Toronto. Distributed by Random House, Inc., New York.

Library of Congress Cataloging in Publication Data
Sorine, Daniel S. Dancershoes.
1. Ballet slippers. 2. Dancers—Interviews.   I. Sorine, Stephanie Riva, joint author. II. Title.
GV1789.2.S66 1979   792.8 ′ 026 79–2156   ISBN 0-394-50665-0   ISBN 0–394–73824–1 pbk.

Manufactured in the United States of America
First Edition

Contents

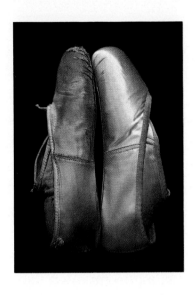

Introduction

Too frequently, a dancer's shoes are taken for granted by the public as simply part of a costume to be put on for dancing. How inaccurate we found this assumption to be! Ballet dancers spend countless hours preparing their shoes by sewing on ribbons and elastics, selecting appropriate ones for a particular ballet or variation, breaking them in, and painting and cleaning them in order to be able to dance with full liberty to apply their talents completely. Although I have been actively involved in the ballet world for more than twenty years, as a dancer and as a teacher, I admit that I was astonished at the extent to which the dancers in this book spontaneously claimed that the quality of their performances were influenced by the state of their shoes. For example, Merrill Ashley said to me, "If the shoes are bad, I can't dance freely, and they can make me feel as if I haven't studied at all," and Carla Fracci said of her shoes, "If something is wrong with them, what I'm dancing can be destroyed." Veronica Tennant exclaimed, "If I happen to have on a really special pair of shoes for a performance, it can make all the difference in the world. All of a sudden I feel that I can tackle anything, and I often actually surprise myself by what I can do." And Mikhail Baryshnikov told me that he treats his ballet slippers like good friends: "I take care of them; otherwise, they will never take care of me." Some other admissions:

"Because some shoes have lumpy, distorted tips, heels that are too long, or shanks that aren't equal in length, I have to treat each shoe individually."
—*Gelsey Kirkland*

"I could not dance classical ballet—above all, the big jumps—without ballet slippers."
—*Valery Panov*

"I don't think I would be a dancer if I didn't dance on pointe."
—*Cynthia Gregory*

"My ballet slippers are definitely the most important article of all my ballet equipment. I couldn't dance—I'd be lost—without them."
—*Peter Martins*

It became increasingly evident to Daniel and me just why these and all the other great dancers I interviewed were so pleased to work with us on this book.

It is well known that ballet dancers are perfectionists about their dancing, and this goes as well for the care and preparation of their shoes. These dancers have much in common; however, each one has developed a particular relationship with his or her shoes. I combined their own words with the personal portraits and shoe photographs that Daniel took to demonstrate how alike—and yet unlike—ballet dancers and their shoes can be.

Dancers' shoes that have been worn are similar to fingerprints; they all have their own characters and identities. This is why Kay Mazzo said, "For the same reason I don't borrow toothbrushes, I wouldn't want to use somebody else's shoes," and Helgi Tomasson said, "It's possible to borrow tights, costumes, or make-up, but never ballet slippers. My slippers must fit and belong to my own feet." You will discover, as we have, that the majority of dancers favor older shoes that bear the impressions of their feet and the steps they have expressed. With only a few exceptions, the dancers' shoes shown in the photographs here have all been danced in on the renowned stages of the world. Imagine the pains and pleasures, the successes and failures, the convictions and even secrets that each shoe has endured!

Just how significant are a ballet dancer's shoes? From working on this book, and from my own experience, I have recognized that dancers may dance, but without a heart and a sole, what they dance cannot be called ballet.

—*Stephanie Riva Sorine*

Merrill Ashley

Mr. Balanchine is one of the few men who is experienced with pointe work; he really understands it. Through his choreography, he's added to pointe technique and increased the possibilities for ballerinas dancing on pointe. He insists that all his classes for women be taken on pointe rather than half-pointe, because he wants each dancer to become familiar with her own particular placement on pointe and to be able to dance in pointe shoes at any speed. So I always take class on pointe; in fact, it's very painful for me to dance on half-pointe, particularly since I tore the ligaments around my bunion.

Ideally a dancer's toes should all be of equal length so that the foot looks square. Mine form a slant, and I basically stand on my big toe. I don't have a great center of balance—I have a tendency to lean inward on my big toe—so I have to shift my weight onto the other toes. When I'm on pointe I have to make these kinds of minor adjustments continually, or else I'll look like a top that has just lost its momentum and is about to go crashing on its side.

Especially since my injury, which didn't heal too well, I need to wear extra-hard pointe shoes for added support. My order consists of strong shanks, hard tips, and high vamps; and because Freed's stock shoes tend to cover the whole foot like a bedroom slipper, I request that the sides be cut down. By specifying the width and depth of the box, I make sure that mine is not too flat, too narrow, or too tapered. I like a big platform; it's better for balancing.

For more than half the ballets I perform, I keep a second pair of shoes ready in the wings, because as soon as the tips of the shoes start to get soft, I must change them.

Otherwise I would stand unevenly and put too much pressure on my big toe. Even in ballets with very little pointe work, I still must wear hard pointe shoes. I break in my shoes very little—only enough so that they aren't slippery on the bottom. Rarely do I warm up in them before a performance—only for a ballet danced to piano music, when I don't want my shoes to make noise.

I brush Fabulon inside the tips of my shoes to keep them hard. I also wrap my toes with paper towels to absorb perspiration, because once the glue, which makes the shoes hard, gets wet, they disintegrate. Once, during a performance in an arena, I was waiting in the wings to go back onstage, and while I was talking to someone I accidentally stepped into a bucket of water. I was lucky that the ballet was almost finished!

I don't have any particular method for sewing on ribbons or a precise spot where I attach them, but I do sew elastics into my ribbons to prevent tendinitis. I wear so many pairs of shoes that it seems as if I spend half my life sewing on ribbons and elastics. During a repertory season, I can go through twenty pairs of shoes a week. Even using a machine, I'm still sewing all the time.

I'm not the kind of person who collects things, but I have saved two pairs of pointe shoes. One pair is from my first solo, and the other is from *Ballo della Regina*, the first ballet Mr. Balanchine created for me as a principal dancer.

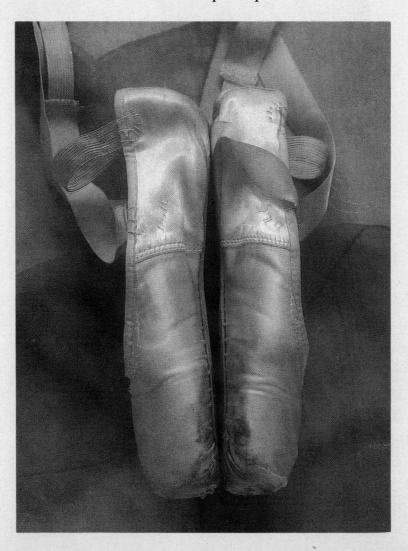

Anthony Dowell

My ballet slippers are made by Gamba, in canvas. I used to wear leather, but funnily enough the canvas ones last longer and keep their shape better. When the canvas gets damp after I've worked in them, the shoes will shrink back into shape, but once the leather is stretched, it stays stretched.

I know exactly how and where the elastics should be sewn and exactly the right amount of tension they should have. It would be very difficult to tell anyone in the theatre, even my dresser, how to do it, although it's something I loathe. In fact, I put it off until my slippers drop off my feet, when of course I must face up to the task of sewing elastics on new slippers.

I have no problem with shoes. I am not like these dancers who go through this terrible business of fussing about this being an inch too long or too short or whatever. I think the boys probably have less trouble than the girls. Over many years, I certainly haven't had any complaints. My ballet slippers arrive, I put them on, and that's that.

Karen Kain

Usually on a good rehearsal day, I wear out a pair of pointe shoes. Even in one hour I can wear out a pair, but it depends on what I'm rehearsing. For something like *Les Sylphides,* I don't wear hard shoes anyway, but *Swan Lake,* which is full of bourrées and pirouettes, wears out my shoes very quickly.

As for performances, once again it depends on the repertoire. In *The Sleeping Beauty* I sometimes use three pairs of pointe shoes, but not brand-new ones. As each act requires a different kind of shoe, each pair has to be broken in in a certain way. Aurora is one role that really frightens me, because the form and the technique are so difficult and there is not a great deal of characterization to fall back on. I cannot fake or hide anything, and therefore I give extra attention to my shoes.

I break my pointe shoes in by practicing in them. With experience, I've come to know how soft I want them. For the second act of *Giselle,* my shoes are super soft, so I can feel the floor through them and don't make any noise. When I was first learning *Giselle,* I looked at pictures of Spessivtzeva and formed an ideal vision of how the second act should look—how the technique should be there but not visible, how the jumps should be very high and the landings very soft, so no effort seems involved.

I like the look of dancing on pointe, and the feeling—except, of course, when the shoes have been on too long and my feet get sore. Actually, I feel more comfortable on pointe than on half-pointe; when I'm dancing on half-pointe, I always find that my ankles twist. Also, there is less friction with the floor when I'm on pointe. I don't want the floor to be slippery, but I also don't want it to have so much resistance that my body goes one way and my foot stays in the same place. Unfortunately, that can happen, and it hurts.

Men would understand more about ballerinas, especially in partnering, if they tried doing a little pointe work themselves. There is a different distribution of weight when you're on pointe, and they could learn how a ballerina wants to be supported and where her weight needs to be.

Valery Panov

The ballet slippers that I will design will be the ones that I will like best. At the moment, I have only a plan. I want the area underneath the toes to be made of leather and the rest of the slipper to be made of a light fabric, perhaps nylon. I am hoping that Capezio will make these for me. Now I dance in leather Capezios, which I special-order with a shorter vamp and thinner soles. Where I sew the elastics on is of great importance to me. I am very strict in placing them crossed over my insteps so that the slippers fit more securely.

Because of their thin soles, my slippers are as light and as flexible as gloves, which is essential for controlling turns. It is especially important that my toes be able to grasp the floor and to stay together during jumps and landings. I could not dance classical ballet—above all, the big jumps—without ballet slippers. Modern dancers, who dance barefoot, cannot do big jumps because they would destroy their toes. And I love to jump. In fact, during my daily morning company class I am sometimes nearly asleep during the barre and will only open my eyes for the jumping combinations.

To perform with new shoes is impossible. Only after two or three rehearsals can I wear them onstage.

Eva Evdokimova

I wouldn't be able to stand on pointe if I had to wear another dancer's shoes. Because I have rather high insteps, I would go completely over the front. When my shoes aren't the right form, particularly the tip, I say, "Send them back!" Twelve out of twenty pairs are sent back regularly.

I sew on my own ribbons, at a special angle to the shoe, and darn the tips a little bit to make a better platform for balancing. For performances I sew the knot of the ribbons to secure against their untying. I don't use elastics—I use rosin to keep the heels from slipping off. To preserve my pointe shoes, I always shellac them.

I still work hard on my pointe technique, as it has not been the easiest of my accomplishments. Jumping was always a lot easier for me. When I was young, my ankles were the weakest part of my body, and I had to work hard to strengthen them. Over the years I have found that the Russian type of class, which includes more strenuous exercises at the barre, longer adagios in the center, and more intricate combinations, is best for getting me into shape. After a class like that, I always feel good and strong and that I can cope with anything in my repertoire. Also, ever since I started dancing *Swan Lake*, I think that my pointe work has been improving, because it is such a demanding ballet. When I do *Swan Lake* a few times in succession, it brings me into shape and position fantastically.

For Classical ballets like *The Sleeping Beauty* and *Swan Lake*, with all their pointe work, I need quite a firm shoe to support my foot. For Romantic ballets like *Giselle*, which require a great deal of jumping, I want the shoes to be light. Every ballet requires a different style, technique, and approach.

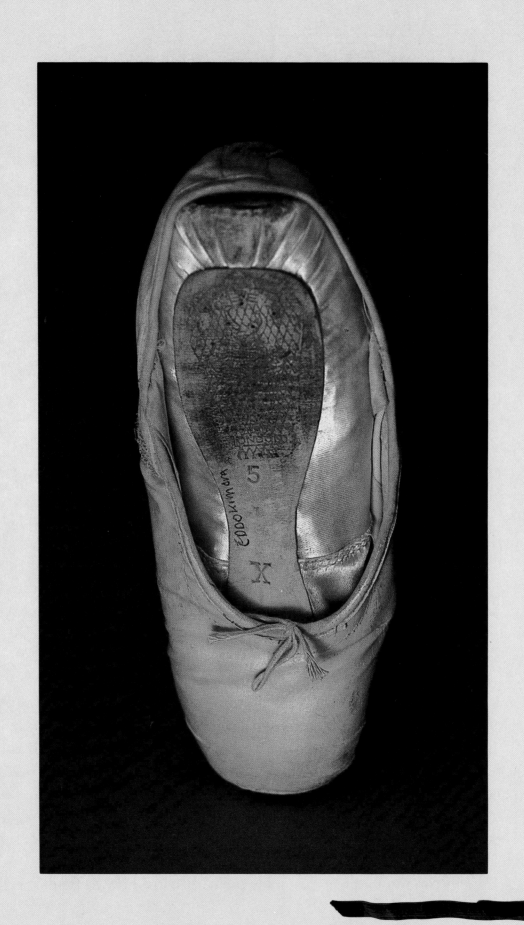

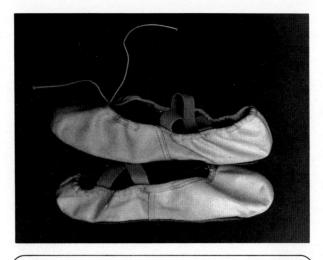

Daniel Duell

Just as scruffy canvas ballet slippers were beginning to be a common (and irritating) sight onstage at the State Theatre, Mr. Balanchine said, "No more canvas!" and stopped ordering canvas shoes for the men in the New York City Ballet. Coincidentally, I was already beginning to prefer leather slippers, because they stay nicer and retain spray paint longer. When I danced in canvas slippers, I constantly felt I was bruising my toes, because the fabric didn't give. However, they did hold their shape until they were completely worn through. Leather shoes are so pliant that you have to stop wearing them when they stretch, because they become blobby and shapeless.

A good pair of ballet slippers helps make my feet look well pointed. The vamps should be neither too short nor too long, the drawstrings elastic, and the sides cut low, especially by the arch. Sometimes, though, the vamps are so short that they don't even cover my bunion; at other times the soles will bunch up underneath or the shoes will just be too small. Although I can dance with bad shoes, it's uncomfortable, inhibiting, and even threatening, because I keep feeling that they're going to pop off.

Once I actually did lose one of my shoes onstage through using only one elastic, and I've been crisscrossing them with two ever since.

I don't think men should perform in toe shoes, but to practice on pointe can be very useful. In fact, a couple of months ago I started doing the barre in company class in toe shoes. Initially I felt very weak and shaky, but it wasn't as painful as I had imagined it would be. Unlike the ballerinas, who dance for hours and hours every day on their toes, I'm only spending half an hour at a time in toe shoes, and I'm not always on pointe during that time. Already there is quite an improvement in how my feet feel and look, and working in toe shoes stretches my feet as nothing else can; and my feet are becoming increasingly flexible.

Dancing on my toes has also made me realize just how difficult it is to do certain steps on pointe—for instance, to do a piqué back and to position the ankle in a supportive way. Now I have an extra awareness and comprehension as a partner.

Veronica Tennant

My instrument is my body, but my pointe shoes are a very important accessory to my profession. When I have a major performance coming up, I spend a few days choosing the right shoes; even though I may only wear two pairs for the performance, I want to have four pairs to choose among. That way I feel confident.

I wear Freed pointe shoes made to my specifications. I ask for the most flexible sole and a good platform to balance on with a tiny bit of support in the block; otherwise my toes would hurt too much, because I'm one of those dancers who never wraps her toes with anything. I like my shoes to be extremely pliable and flexible; what I seek are pointe shoes that are almost like gloves and give the foot total freedom. I want to achieve the look that the ballerinas have in the old lithographs, where the foot looks like an extension of the leg.

I break in my shoes by bending them in half, stepping on them, and wetting them. Water dissolves the glue that makes the pointe shoe stiff; by wetting the heel and halfway up the arch—sometimes even a little bit into the block—I get the shoes completely malleable. I keep the water away from the tips, to leave them as hard as possible. I experiment with everything to keep the tips hard. Now I'm testing contact cement.

I've often wondered about what would happen if I had to wear another dancer's shoes. I suppose that in an emergency I could wear someone else's shoes if there were similarities in our requirements, but I would have trouble with a very heavy shoe.

I used to think that it was all in the shoes, but now I realize that everything I do is in my head. Nevertheless, if I happen to have on a really special pair of shoes for a performance, it can make all the difference in the world. All of a sudden I feel that I can tackle anything, and I often actually surprise myself by what I can do.

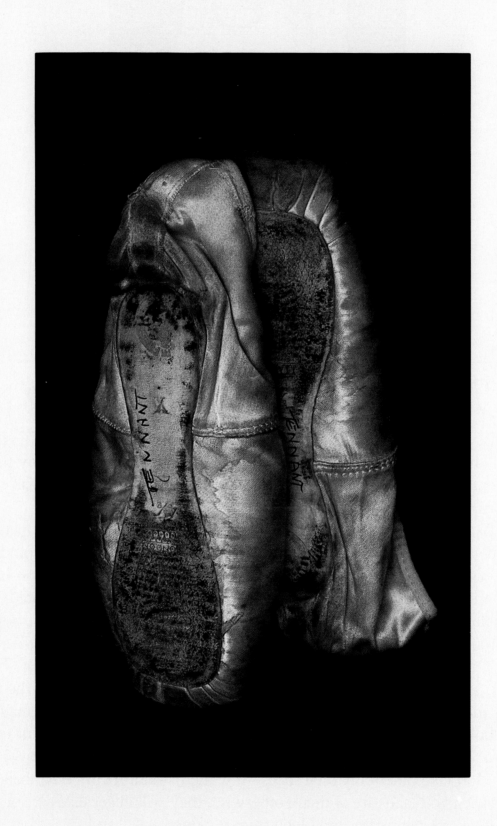

Mikhail Baryshnikov

Thank God I don't remember what I thought when I put on my first pair of ballet slippers as a young boy. I don't want to remember. There is a Russian saying for such situations: it was a long time ago and not true.

My teachers in Russia didn't describe specifically how ballet slippers must fit, but it is simply logical that the foot should feel comfortable and the shoe shouldn't be too small or too big. How the shoe should be shaped to be suitable for work on half-pointe depends on the construction of one's toes. Also, when the foot is pointed, the shoe shouldn't be floppy at the tips and the sole under the arch should be right next to the foot so that the profile of the arch can be seen.

I am now wearing English slippers made by Gamba in leather. They are a special order, a special design, but they are quite normal as slippers. I like them because they are soft and comfortable. The best shoes, I think, are the Russian ones made in Moscow for the Bolshoi Ballet. They are made from very light canvas and are cut to conform thoroughly to the foot, as a fine glove is cut for the hand. But in the West, I favor Gambas.

Do I take care of my own shoes—sew them, paint them? Well, ballet slippers are like good friends. I take care of them; otherwise, they will never take care of me. But I hate to sew; it takes a lot of time, and blood from my fingers.

New shoes are painful. Although I break in my own shoes, I would prefer to give them to someone else to do. For me, comparatively big, stretched-out shoes are the most agreeable. In fact, I don't like them snug at all; I can't dance in them. Onstage I have to wear very old, worn shoes.

How long my shoes will last varies from season to season. Sometimes they last for years, because they might be for a ballet that I do not perform more than once a year. The pair that I wear for *Le Spectre de la Rose* I have had already for three years. But shoes often only last for one performance. Dancing on a linoleum floor that has been painted seems to cause shoes to wear the fastest.

I depend a great deal on my shoes; they can definitely influence a performance. Basically, when my feet are not comfortable and are irritated, this disturbs me the most, and naturally it bothers me if I don't give a good performance. However, I have continued in performances with shoes that were splitting on the sides or from which the soles were separating, even though it was not too pleasant. Funny things have happened onstage, but fortunately I have never lost a shoe.

I never tried to stand on my toes—thank God!—but I've seen men dance on pointe: in Russia the Georgian folk dancers, and here in New York, Les Ballets Trockadero de Monte Carlo. (I think it is hysterically funny, but it's really a question of taste.)

If dancing on pointe works for the choreography, why shouldn't men do it? I saw a ballet in Russia called *Faun and Nymph*. The male dancer who represented the faun was on pointe, and he truly looked like a faun with hoofs. It was positively spectacular!

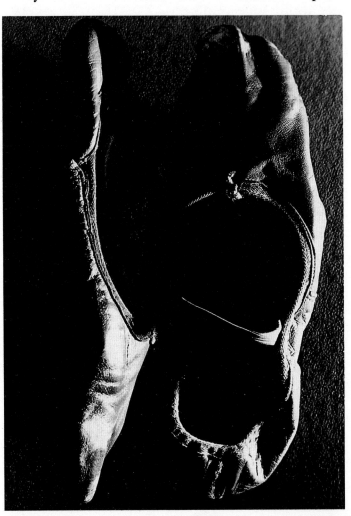

Francesca Corkle

When I was about four years old, I used to do a very bad thing. Because I wanted to dance on pointe so much, I'd stuff tissues inside my ballet slippers and do relevés and little poses on pointe around the house. My mother, who is a ballet teacher, would tell me not to do this because I could ruin my feet, but as soon as she turned around, I was back on my toes. As a result of the pressure, I now have calcium deposits on my big toe where a bunion normally is, except that it protrudes on top of the foot instead of to the side. My father was a radiologist, and he brought me to his clinic, where he took X-rays to study my physical development. When I was ten, my parents decided I was ready to dance on pointe with the proper training from my mother.

I don't need to depend on my shoes for support; I like a softer shoe, to feel that I'm dancing on pointe on my own. Rarely do I wear hard shoes; only for a ballet like *Petrouchka*, in which there are a lot of hops on pointe. If I have three ballets to perform in one evening, I'll do those ballets in one pair of shoes. By cleaning my shoes with a face cloth moistened with Carbona and applying a thin coat of pink shoe polish, I can keep my shoes clean. This also takes the sheen off the satin.

When I go to the showroom, I ask for the lightest shoe possible—no extra shanking or anything, just a simple shoe. Unless one has an extreme foot problem, I feel it is better not to complicate things. Actually, I think it is a bit neurotic how dancers bother about their shoes. On the other hand, there have been times during performances when I wished I could run off the stage—when I had shoes that didn't fit and felt like foreign objects. All my thoughts would go to my feet, and my philosophy of dancing on pointe is to get my thoughts *away* from my feet. I must be light when I dance, and if I'm constantly thinking about my shoes, my performance will be earthbound.

Frank Augustyn

I didn't have much luck with leather slippers, because as I pointed my foot the leather buckled around and underneath the toes. So now I wear canvas slippers, made by Repetto. I usually prefer them with a very high vamp and a rather wide sole, as I find I work better with a broader base.

Being comfortable in my ballet slippers has a psychological effect on me. I'm more willing to try different steps when I'm more at ease, because I don't have to worry about how my slippers fit. Similarly, if a girl finds a good pair of pointe shoes that she can balance in, turn in, perhaps even jump in, and that don't make a lot of noise, she feels much more comfortable and free. After all, ballet dancers try to appear ethereal, as if they are flying. Women achieve this quality by rising on pointe and by being lifted by men; men achieve it by turning and jumping. The higher they jump, the longer they can sustain that impression, that picture in the air. This is why I wear a comfortable pair of slippers until the canvas splits. New shoes have a tendency to be a little too tight and painful for me; it takes about a week of daily classes for me to feel settled and comfortable enough in new slippers.

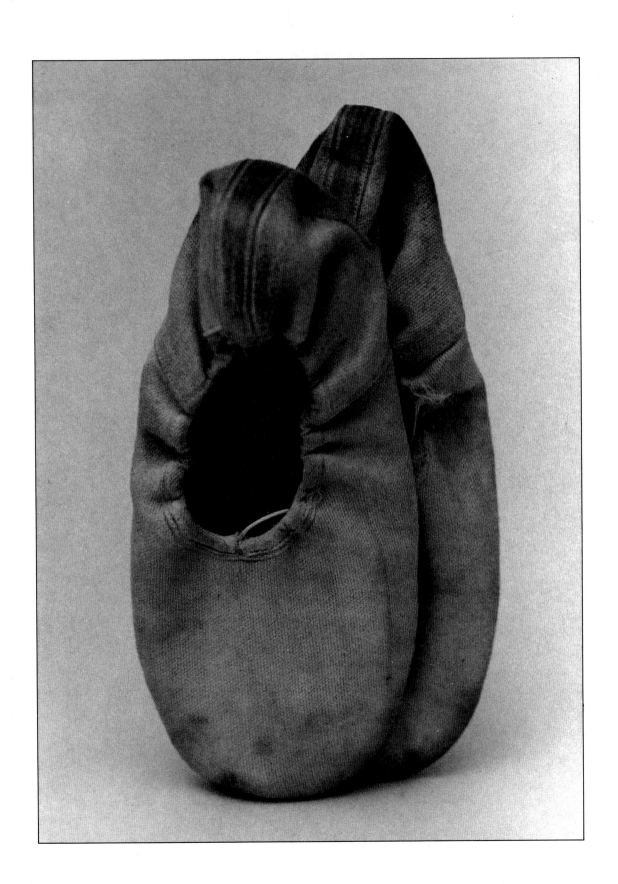

Liliana Belfiore

Pointe shoes are a necessity for classical ballet. There really isn't any excuse for having bad shoes; it's the dancer's responsibility to have good ones available. To prepare my shoes I first sew on ribbons at a specific angle, and then I crush the box with my hands. I don't bend the sole at all. Occasionally Gamba will send me a pair of shoes that are too short in the heel, and I need to sew on elastics in the back of the shoe to lace my ribbons through, which pulls the heel higher up on my foot. It's too much work to darn the tips, so when the shoes are getting old and the satin on the tips begins to fray, I just keep trimming it.

Since I have a high instep, I order a long vamp. Compared with the other makes of shoes, which always tortured my feet and broke very quickly, my Gamba shoes are comfortable and sturdy. Quite often, one pair of Gambas will be strong enough for two or three performances. Ballets like *Giselle* and *Swan Lake*, which include both adagio and allegro movements, usually require both hard and soft shoes. For those types of ballets, I wear two or even three pairs for each performance.

Shoes are important, but I never place that much importance on them. They must fulfill a function, feel all right, and look nice. I will clean my shoes when they are dirty, but I will not worship them.

It's true that pointe shoes can affect a performance, but I can dance anyway when I have bad shoes, although my feet may not look so pretty. Unlike some dancers, who blame objects if they dance poorly, I don't say, "My shoes are rotten," or, "My hair is ugly," or whatever. If I lose my balance or can't turn, I know it's an off day for me, and I just hope I'll be in better shape for the next performance.

George de la Peña

By watching other dancers and observing what they did with their slippers and how they were meant to look, I learned what to do for myself. I actually hated my first ballet slippers; I felt ridiculous in them. The drawstrings were tied in little bows in the front, and the shoes were so huge that I probably could have used them to float in the Central Park lake.

Since I wear the same size as Mikhail Baryshnikov, years ago he gave me a pair of his Russian shoes to try. I liked them because I had a better feel for the floor and more traction than with the shoes I had been wearing. Rather than having a thick sole underneath my toes as a surface, I felt almost as if my toes were the actual surface. When Mischa ordered shoes in this Russian style from Gamba in London, I requested the identical order. Because the slippers fit so well, they almost feel like a part of my foot. They're kidskin, with a slightly higher vamp and a shorter and narrower sole than the standard Gamba shoe.

Many times I've alternated between canvas and leather slippers. Leather is more comfortable, because it stretches and expands to conform to my foot; but canvas gives a different look to the line of the leg. The leather is shinier and more distinct, whereas the canvas makes the foot continue the line of the leg because the shoe is not as pronounced. Fortunately, Gamba's leather is not that shiny, and the spray paint used to change the color of the shoes dulls the shine further.

It's not steps that destroy the slippers as much as floors, although in general the floors I dance on are excellent. Still, now and then I have to dance on wood. Turning on a wooden floor annihilates my shoes. In Athens I performed in the Herod Atticus Theatre, which has a Masonite stage, and when I did a few pirouettes, my shoe split open, at which point I was in a desperate situation. Luckily my wardrobe people were in the wings ready to help, and they quickly sewed elastics onto a new pair of slippers. Since that time, I have always kept an extra pair of shoes in the wings (with the elastics already attached) in case something happens.

Toward the end of the day, when my feet begin to swell, I change from ballet slippers to character shoes. These have a low heel, and so some of the pressure on my feet and legs is alleviated. I don't do class in character shoes—they're too cumbersome—but I do wear them any other time and for rehearsals in which they won't interfere with the choreography or the technique.

Kay Mazzo

Aesthetically, a dancer looks nicer on pointe than on half-pointe, because her line is extended and her arch is presented. Pointe shoes are fashioned in the best possible way to show off a dancer's foot, making it look elongated and giving it a pretty line. The satin reflects light and accentuates the line of the foot. I like them shiny rather than dull, because that way the foot doesn't mix in with the tights.

One word that immediately comes to mind when I think about pointe shoes is "light." It's crucial that I have a very lightweight shoe. Anything that feels like a pointe shoe, I don't want. I must feel that I'm the one who is doing the dancing, not the shoes.

I order basic stock shoes from Capezio, although I do need two different sizes because my feet are not the same length. When I want the arch to be more flexible, I soften it with my hands; when I want a harder arch, I pick out shoes that are firmer in that area. Pointe shoes are not all constructed identically, and I prefer it that way—otherwise I wouldn't be able to choose the different shoes I need for particular ballets.

According to my podiatrist, most of my current foot troubles were caused by tight pointe shoes and excessive pointe work. I had a bone spur removed from my big toe, and I used to have two bones that crossed over on the top of my arch from dancing on pointe when I was only eight years old, which was too young. They finally uncrossed and went back into place. I have also acquired a chronic Achilles' tendon problem, mainly from the action of going up on pointe and down again so many times each day.

Although I don't like to wear hard pointe shoes for performances, to dance in Balanchine's *Square Dance* they are a necessity. Not only don't I have time to change shoes during the ballet, but by the time it's over, the shoes are completely worn out. For *Square Dance* I simply put on my shoes, which aren't broken in, get out onstage, and dance.

Frank Andersen

This pair of Løve ballet slippers that I'm wearing is one of the last pairs of Løve shoes ever, and this is a catastrophe, because shoes that are completely handmade like these are rare. I've never had another brand of ballet slippers that made me feel as if I were without shoes, as these do. They are just like gloves.

Løve has a villa outside of Copenhagen, where he had been working all of his life. He worked alone in his miniature factory, and as far back as I can remember, he made most of the shoes for the Royal Danish Ballet. Unfortunately, Løve is getting very old, and he had a heart attack. All of the dancers who used his shoes had to find new ones immediately. Luckily, I had saved enough to last me one more season.

Years ago Løve decided what kind of special order I required by studying a drawing he made of my foot. He gave me a medium-length vamp, because a vamp that is too long ruins the angle of my instep when I'm on half-pointe, and one that is too short irritates my toe knuckles. He had all different kinds of materials, so I could choose whatever I wanted. I chose a very soft but strong material so that my shoes wouldn't stretch out ten sizes bigger within two days. As a result, my shoes stay on my feet very well, and I don't have to position my elastics too far back. I sew them on with a sewing machine, always at the same place. Generally, I do ten pairs at a time.

The Royal Danish Ballet's treasure is the Bournonville repertoire. The exact style and tradition of these ballets has been preserved, and I love to dance in them. For these Bournonville programs the male dancers wear the traditional shoes, which are black with a split of white on the vamp. Ever since Bournonville choreographed his ballets, more than one hundred and fifty years ago, this design of ballet slipper has been used.

Nadia Potts

When I first joined the National Ballet of Canada, I received marvelous shoes. But then slowly the shipments began to become defective; some shoes were a half-size too small or too large, and the tips were all bumpy. I was having a terrible time. Then, on tour in San Francisco, Karen Kain was approached by a representative from Schachtner. She was curious, so she tried their shoes and then recommended them to the rest of us. I went to the showroom and was delighted to find a shoe I could wear.

Unlike other shoes I've tried, which give me the feeling I'm standing on a thick sole, the soles on Schachtners lie absolutely flat on the ground. They are also fabulously light and seem to last forever, due to the material they are made of, which contains fiber glass. Since I have begun wearing Schachtner shoes, I find I need very few pairs. Although I usually use a new pair of shoes for each *Sleeping Beauty* or *Swan Lake*, I have done three performances of *Swan Lake* in one pair of pointe shoes.

However, they do take a long time to break in, and they can be quite noisy. I have to spend an hour preparing my shoes and at least another hour practicing or rehearsing in them before I can go onstage. If I'm dancing in the second act of *Giselle*, I will soak the shoes in alcohol, and jam them in a door every night for a week, until they are soft enough. I can rehearse in any old shoes, but for a performance I am always much fussier.

Some of the dancers in the National Ballet of Canada darn the tips of their shoes, but I crochet small toe caps and glue them to the tips. This makes a sturdier platform to stand on, and I can control my feet better, so that I don't roll over onto my big toe, especially on my right foot. The toe caps also help to quiet the noise of the shoes, along with the piece of moleskin that I sew onto the pleats.

In many instances it is the shoes that are the problem and not the actual steps on pointe. When I have a good pair of shoes, everything is so straightforward that it is a pleasure to dance. If dancers could always have perfect shoes, it would be fantastic!

Christian Holder

Canvas ballet slippers made by Capezio are the shoes I dance in most often, although I also wear character shoes, sneakers, and boots. Each shoe has its own vocabulary of steps and its own distinct style; in Jerome Robbins' *New York Export: Opus Jazz*, it would be strange to dance in ballet slippers, as it was choreographed for sneakers.

If I'm wearing character shoes, I break them in, or if I feel that I need to have more contact with the floor in a particular ballet, I make sure I have older shoes available. However, I can put on new shoes and go directly onstage in ballets like *Moves* and *Brouillards*. How long they last depends on the ballet.

I could use another dancer's shoes if it were a necessity and they were the right size, but they would probably not be as comfortable as my own. What makes my slippers especially suitable for my feet is that the heel reaches further up to my Achilles' tendon and they have elastic drawstrings, which can be taut and yet still give. When my shoes fit well, I can forget them, and create a better relationship with the floor.

Nothing should be obvious about a man's ballet slippers. The elastics are sewn across the instep to keep the shoes on, not for decoration. In the photograph on the facing page, my elastics are noticeable because they're white and I'm not wearing the white socks that are supposed to be worn with them in *Cakewalk*.

When I have a performance, I try to keep clear of outside vibes. By getting into my costume myself and taking care of my ballet shoes, I feel that I'm in touch with everything that's on my body, and this helps me to build the character of the role.

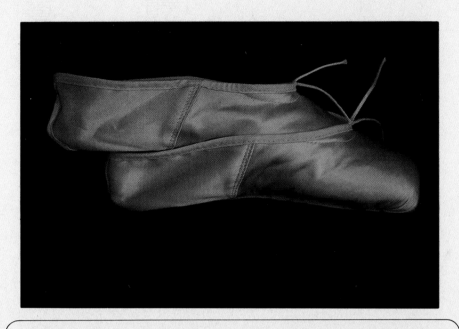

Natalia Makarova

Here in America, I find I'm using a greater number of pointe shoes. In Russia I would have a total of four performances in a whole month; during a season of American Ballet Theatre I may perform every other day—sometimes more. For this period of my career, I think it's much better.

I special-order my shoes from Freed, but even so, out of ten pairs I can only find one that will be really comfortable and suitable for performance. In fact, even before I put them on I can already see which ones will not fit well. When the box seems to point up instead of down, it will be very disturbing aesthetically and give the impression that I'm not fully stretching my toes. Dancing in comfortable pointe shoes that fit well is extremely important. Everything else is up to the ballerina, but not the pointe shoes.

As I cannot stand noisy pointe shoes, I try to get rid of the noise. I squeeze the box by closing a door on it. (I've probably broken all the doors in Europe, and now I'm breaking them in America.) The shoes will also become soft and noiseless by hammering the box with a special hammer or by simply wearing them for a long time.

Especially for Romantic ballets like *Giselle* and *Les Sylphides*, when I want to appear totally light, I have to wear completely worn, very old, soft, and flexible pointe shoes, so that it's almost like standing on my toes on my own. Because I have a high arch and a high instep, I often need to sew extra threads across the vamp for added support; otherwise I will go over too much on my toes. I avoid danger by rubbing rosin on the ends of my ribbons and on the heels of my tights; that way my ribbons don't untie and the heels don't shift up and down as I dance.

Robert Weiss

Being able to feel the floor underneath my toes while I'm dancing is essential, because the floor must be utilized. As there is a tremendous amount of friction between the foot and the floor, I wouldn't particularly want to dance barefoot. Ballet slippers protect the feet while allowing the toes to be sensitive to the floor's surface, because there isn't any sole under the toes—only pleating.

The leather of the slippers should be smooth and even; I know that the leather that is regularly used could be improved. There's a wonderful craftsman in Denmark who works with the softest leather; I tried a pair of his shoes, and they were the best I ever had.

I order elastic drawstrings instead of cotton. With elastic the shoes fit closer, because the usual gaps that form at the sides of the shoes when you go on half-pointe are eliminated. Also, the elastic doesn't pinch the back of my heel as the cotton does.

My shoes conform to my feet from working and perspiring in them. I normally just put my slippers on and wear them, but if I have an important role to dance, I might do some extra warm-ups to break them in. A pair of shoes normally lasts two or three performances. The wardrobe mistresses refuse to sew on elastics. I could get one of the girls to help, but I would rather do it myself. Knowing that my elastics are stable gives me added confidence and freedom in performance.

Gamba is the name of the company that makes my ballet slippers. Generally all the pairs I get are alike; they are all good, never too stiff or too tight. My slippers might not affect the quality of my performance; nevertheless, it's essential that I be comfortable in them when I'm dancing.

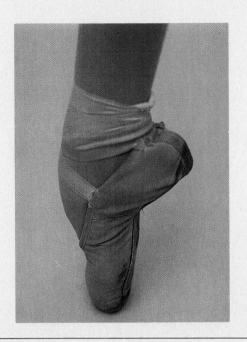

Christine Sarry

I can break in a pair of pointe shoes and twelve months later still be wearing them. Because I basically stand straight on my toes, as opposed to knuckling over or pressing down in the tips of my shoes, my weight is lifted and I'm much lighter on the shoe. When I rise on pointe, I gain a couple of inches in height, which is an advantage, since I'm quite short—only five feet two. I feel that I'm blessed in having long feet; as a matter of fact, some dancers who are five feet six wear my pointe shoe size.

Having danced barefoot, in tennis shoes, in boots, in character shoes, and in ballet slippers, I can honestly say that I prefer dancing in pointe shoes. But I hate breaking in new shoes—I just detest it. I can't tolerate the sound of new, hard pointe shoes onstage, so I put alcohol on them and have one of the boys in the company stamp on them to flatten down the box. After dancing through an entire rehearsal period of four to five weeks—if Eliot is choreographing a new ballet, several months—I'll use those shoes for a ballet in which *hard* shoes are needed! My hard shoes would be considered devastated by most dancers. That "hard" pair will be used throughout the repertoire to become soft enough for the ballets in which I hardly need any shoe at all, like *Intermezzo*.

I always loved to look at photographs of Mia Slavenska, mostly because she didn't have any ribbons on her shoes. I especially dislike the look of satin ribbons, which seem to break the line of the leg. Because of this, I didn't mind it when my teacher, Carmelita Maracci, suggested that I switch to twill tape when I was thirteen years old. (Twill tape is used for sewing hems.) Not only is the matte finish of the twill ribbons prettier for the line of the foot, since they seem to melt into the tights, but they also stay securely wrapped around the ankles without slipping. To blend them even more, I dab powder on my ribbons, tights, and shoes. One of my mother's sweetest contributions to my career is her dyeing the twill tape pink, as it comes only in white. She buys it in bulk and sends it to me from California. This gives my shoes a special and unusual touch. People sitting in the first rows of the audience have often asked me if I had ribbons on my shoes. They could not understand it, but they admired the illusion.

After establishing which shoe will be my right one and which will be my left, I mark it on the soles. I also write on the soles little notes, like "blisters" or the name of the last ballet the shoes were worn for, to keep track of the steps the shoes know. When I was guesting with the Royal Winnipeg Ballet in Canada, I had a terrible experience. During *La Fille Mal Gardée* one side of my shoe separated from the sole. As soon as I had an exit, I asked someone to go to my dressing room to get another pair of shoes. He accidentally picked up two left shoes, and due to the darkness in the wings and the desperation of my situation, I wasn't aware of his mistake until the shoes were on my feet and it was too late to do anything. Naturally, I felt as though I had two left feet. I had to go back onstage and perform hops on pointe, which were nearly impossible and extremely uncomfortable!

Bart Cook

Although my feet are manageable, they aren't the world's best, with their high insteps, high arches, and square-shaped toes. To strengthen my feet, I tried doing some pointe work, but I found it excruciating because I have an enormous big toe. Merrill Ashley has toes shaped like mine, and I don't know how she can dance. When I tried standing on pointe, I couldn't bear the pain; in fact, if I had to dance on pointe, I wouldn't be a dancer. Because of the unusual slant of my toes, I put off breaking in new shoes, as it is such an ordeal to stretch out the leather surrounding the longest toes. Once I tried a shoe a size larger; this allowed more space for my big toe, but the leather bagged horribly around the smaller toes. I even tried stuffing the shoes, but the stuffing kept moving around and lumping. I am also quite lazy, so I wear my slippers until they fall apart.

To make the Capezio slippers conform to the irregularities of my foot, I cut some material away, twist the shoes in knots, and rub the leather with alcohol. Alcohol can destroy the surface of the leather, but the slippers are painted for most performances, and this covers the damage.

The knot of the elastic drawstrings used to rub across my toe knuckles, causing perpetual scabs, so I changed my order. Now the ends of the drawstrings meet at the sides of the shoes instead of in the front. The drawstrings cannot be pulled too tight or else the circulation in the foot will be cut off. To keep the shoes on my feet, along with crossed elastics over my insteps I either put rosin on the heels of my tights or sew the heels of my slippers to my tights. In *Agon* the rosin method is not sufficient; I do steps that involve dragging my heels on the floor, and to do these steps fully, with all of my energy, I absolutely cannot have any fears about my shoes slipping off.

My slippers have Teknik soles, which are lightweight and thin. Still, depending on the condition of the corns on the bottoms of my feet and how well the shoes are made, I often find it necessary to undo the soles from the pleating, trim away some of the rough edges, and sew them back together again. The pressure from my big toe tends to pull the stitches out so that the leather flaps around in front of the shoe, which can be hazardous. I call this a blowout because it looks just like a flat tire.

Martine van Hamel

Even though my ankles are strong, they're very flexible, and I need a sturdy shoe for added support. This is why I wear Schachtners. Also, they're very durable—I need only two or three pairs a week for rehearsals.

Jumping is particularly strenuous in hard pointe shoes, because I need more power in my foot for added control. To jump and to do quick movements in pointe shoes requires more energy from the feet; therefore, when I do Myrtha in *Giselle*, or *La Sylphide*, with its many jumps, I try to have shoes that are very broken in. I am constantly working to have my entire foot use the floor, so I need softer shoes. To dance Glen Tetley's choreography, which is based on classical ballet technique but also includes sculptural movements, I also use softer shoes. They enable me to maintain the continuity of the movement, going through positions and forming and molding shapes with my body.

Although it's necessary to take vacations, I can't just take time off and expect to come back in the same shape I was in when I left. I always get punished in some way for relaxing. Dancing on pointe is the most difficult part to get back to, because I must toughen and strengthen my feet again. After I've been on vacation, I tend to wear out my pointe shoes faster than when I'm in good shape; when my feet are stronger, the shoes hold together longer, since I don't put as much pressure down in the toes. It's a little painful, and I sort of wish I didn't have to dance on pointe; but once I get over the discomfort, it's nice. It lengthens my line just that ideal bit more.

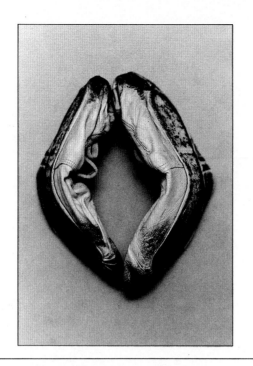

Mel Tomlinson

Since 1973 I've gone from a size 12 Capezio ballet slipper to a size 9. I'm not going any lower than that—in fact, my shoes are so tight now that if my feet could talk, they would scream, "Let me out!" It was not my idea to wear such small slippers; Arthur Mitchell, the director of the Dance Theatre of Harlem, insisted. The tighter the shoe, he figured, the more I would have to point my foot for any comfort. And it worked! Now I have developed arches. Unfortunately, my tight shoes have also caused calcium deposits to accumulate on my toe joints, and I've developed arthritis, which mostly distresses me when it snows. (If you want to know when it's going to snow, I can tell you.)

There have been times when the skin on my toe knuckles puffs up and rubs off against the leather; inside the shoe I can sense it, and sometimes the blood will leak through. Not too long ago my feet resembled my brother's—pinkish and soft. These days my feet are calloused, knotty, and rough. It's worth all this pain to me now, in order to please the audience with my dancing, but for the future...all I'll be left with are memories—and pain.

My shoes stay on pretty well without elastics, and I would prefer not to use them. Nevertheless, for security I do sew elastics on my slippers. At first I was trying to be very fashionable, with crisscrossed elastics like Nureyev, but this didn't agree with me. A wide elastic bound my foot too much, so now I use narrow elastics, one across each instep. Sometimes I even sew my shoes to my socks or tights—anything to prevent them from flying off!

If I want to wear an old pair of slippers, I have to pour water into them to allow the leather to readjust to my present bumps and curves. At the same time, the water refreshes my toes—like quenching a thirst.

Carla Fracci

It depends on the ballet, but usually I like my pointe shoes to be hard, in order to support the foot. Occasionally they will be too hard, especially underneath the toes, and I must bang the shoes on the floor to soften them and to get rid of the noise. By working in class and rehearsing on pointe, and with the help of some rosin, I form the shoe to the shape of my foot. Dancing on pointe is easier in a way for me than dancing on half-pointe, because the muscles get less tired. But I also work on half-pointe in class because it makes me stronger.

I don't want my feet to look as if they're rolling over the front of the box, but I do use softer shoes for ballets such as *Giselle* and *La Sylphide*. To dance Aurora in *The Sleeping Beauty* I wear harder shoes. In the first act of *Giselle* I wear softer shoes for the first part and change to a stronger pair for the variation.

It's very important to me to have the right shoes. If something is wrong with them, what I'm dancing can be destroyed. I keep an extra pair of pointe shoes in the wings at all times, ready if something should happen.

When they are really ruined after a performance, I give my pointe shoes to the people who ask me for them or I use them for class. I did save the pair I wore for my first big performance—*Pas de Quatre* with Alicia Markova, Yvette Chauviré, and Margrethe Schanne in Nervi during the 1957 festival there. To be close to these wonderful dancers at so young an age was a tremendous experience. Those are the only shoes that I have saved, and my mother has them.

Patrick Bissell

When I first began studying ballet, like the other boys in my class who didn't know any better, I went to the store and bought ballet slippers as large as my street shoes. One day my teacher said to the class, "You should always buy slippers that are so tight that you can hardly get your feet into them." Because I adored him, whatever he said I treated as gospel; so I bought the smallest shoes I could fit my feet into. It's unbelievable to me now, but they were almost half the size I actually needed. Of course, I developed welts and painful blisters on the backs of my heels, so I hated wearing ballet slippers.

Now I like wearing ballet slippers. I like the sole and the tightness of the metatarsals being held together; and yet I don't like to feel that I have anything on my feet. My feet should be free, and the audience should be able to see as much of my foot as it can. Shoe manufacturers should use as little material as possible—just enough to keep the shoe on the foot and to protect the ball of the foot and the heel. It would also be great to have a shoe made of a material that has the texture and lightness of canvas but that didn't shred in three or four days.

I've worn Capezios for most of my career, and since I have an extremely wide foot, I require a special order of canvas slippers. I usually get an inch taken off the front, sides, and back, and I order a medium-length vamp. If the vamp is too high, I feel restricted when I point my foot or rise on half-pointe; and since the foot is pointed every time it leaves the floor, it's better if it isn't such an effort to do it.

Because they shred and fall apart and it's too much trouble to repaint them, canvas slippers last only a few days. My left shoe wears out faster, because I do more turns on that foot. When the rosin builds up on the sole of the slippers and the weather is hot and humid, which causes the floor to become sticky, I can rip the sole from the pleats within two days. Ideally there should be as little friction as possible for turns. Although I would prefer to wear leather shoes, because I can really grab and push off the floor to jump high in them, I just can't turn in leather. I find that I get stuck because the leather grips the floor too much compared with the canvas, which is more slippery.

I've often wondered why boys don't begin working on pointe from a young age to develop strength in their feet and to gain an additional skill. Because of the speed that can be attained on pointe, a whole new technique for male dancing could be developed. Imagine a powerful turner like Peter Schaufuss in pointe shoes! He could come onstage, prepare for a turn, and continue the turn for the entire variation; possibly he could keep turning in place for ninety-six counts!

Elisabetta Terabust

I stand on my first three toes in my Freed pointe shoes, which have a specially ordered square box and high vamp. At certain times it's terribly painful to stand on pointe, especially in hot, humid weather. Nevertheless, it's easier for me to dance on pointe than on half-pointe, especially when I have to do pirouettes, which I cannot do very well anyway.

For *Romeo and Juliet* I need to use two pairs of shoes—also for *The Sleeping Beauty.* In these ballets and others, I will often need to change my shoes during the performance. That's why I don't sew the knot of my ribbons or glue my heel to my tights. Instead, I rub my heel in rosin before I put my shoes on and also put a little rosin on the ends of my ribbons to keep the knot from untying. I never sew elastics on my pointe shoes, because they seem to cut off the circulation in my feet.

I never dance in completely new shoes. Before putting them on, I pour some shellac inside and do some exercises in them; that way they will take their form from my feet. When I have a good pair (and sometimes I have horrible ones), I try to preserve them by cleaning them with pancake make-up and rehardening them with shellac.

I think it would be beneficial for men to do exercises on pointe to gain extra strength in their feet. When I was studying ballet in Rome, I remember that twice a week the men did exercises on pointe. But I have to admit I thought it was pretty funny.

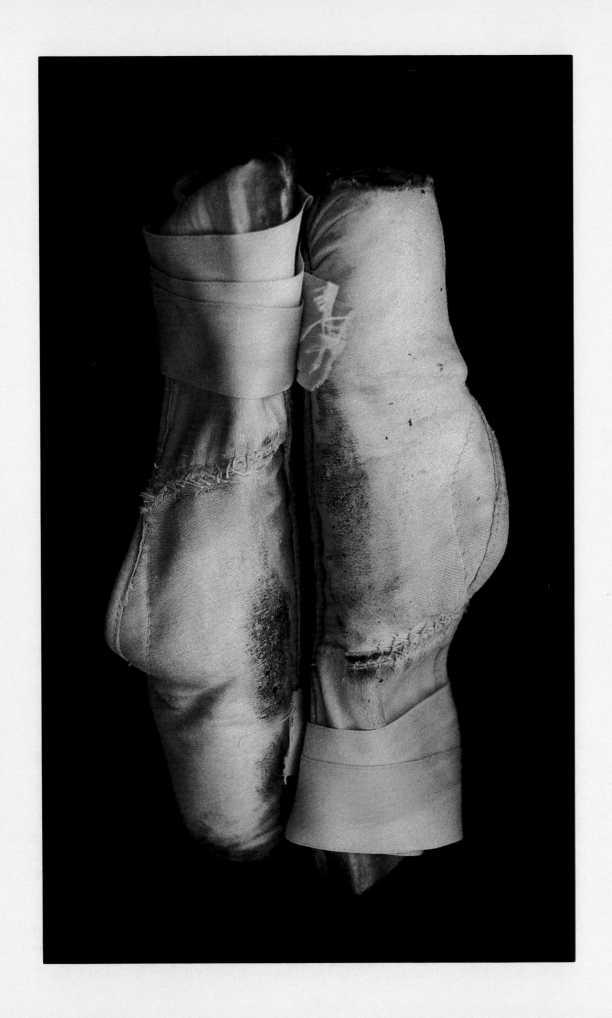

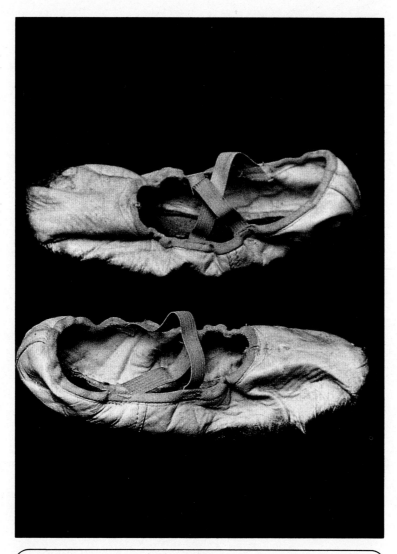

Peter Schaufuss

These glove-soft leather slippers are from Denmark, and they were made specifically for my feet. I've always worn the same kind of slippers—I've never even tried any other brand. My parents, who were both in the Royal Danish Ballet, wore handcrafted ballet shoes made by a Danish man, and ever since I was seven years old and a student in the Royal Danish Ballet school, the same shoemaker has been making mine also. I never thought about changing the style of my shoes or the brand, because I was so content. Unfortunately, he is sick and has stopped making shoes. Now I have to try samples of different factory slippers to find which one suits me best.

Part of being a professional is not being put off by small things. If there isn't anyone to preside over a rehearsal or to teach a class, I can take care of myself. Similarly, I don't let my slippers or any other dance footwear affect my dancing. However, I do avoid tending to my own ballet slippers; the wardrobe personnel do it for me—thank God!

Cynthia Gregory

I usually wear a newly broken-in pair of pointe shoes for classical ballets. I prefer new shoes because they seem to hold my feet together better, and my balance is more secure in them. For more modern ballets, I'll wear softer shoes.

Because I generally like strong pointe shoes that will last a long time, I order my shoes from Schachtner in Vienna. Unlike some pointe shoes, which get very soft and won't reharden, Schachtners will reharden if they are allowed to "rest" for a day or two.

Many ballerinas hammer their pointe shoes, and although I used to think that was sort of silly, it does help to break them in, and recently I've started using the hammer. After I hammer the box a little, I put the shoe on and pour a bit of alcohol on it. To really flatten the point of the shoe in order to make a better platform to balance on, I do a series of relevés, turns, and piqués.

I would never let anyone—not even my mother—sew my ribbons on my shoes; I have to depend on myself to do it. Maybe it's a bit superstitious, but I feel that I have to be the only one responsible for it.

I've been dancing on pointe since I was seven years old, which was too young. In any case, I feel very much at home in pointe shoes and there are some steps I can do on pointe that I could never do on half-pointe. I don't think I would be a dancer if I didn't dance on pointe. When I practice in ballet slippers, I feel awkward and just don't do the steps as well as I would if I were on pointe. And my partners notice how I feel so much heavier on half-pointe. Dancing on pointe seems to pull me up, and I use my muscles more effectively. I actually feel ten pounds lighter when I'm on pointe.

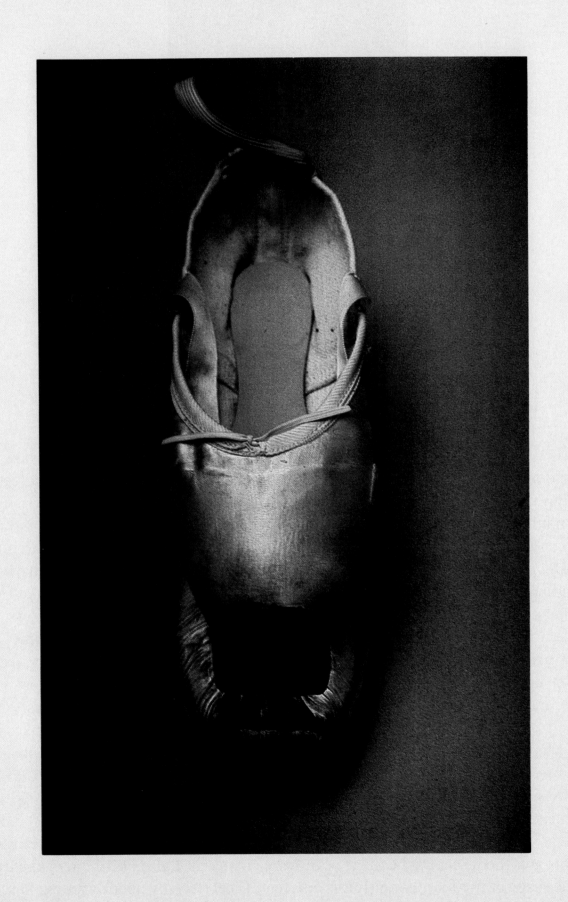

Jean-Pierre Bonnefous

Having never spoken to other dancers about shoes, I don't know how they care for them. I wrap my feet in plastic to keep them warm, stuff my wrapped feet into new slippers, and then wet my shoes completely with water. By doing a barre in wet shoes and then letting them dry on my feet, I mold them to my foot's contours. Now and then I cut away about half an inch from the middle of the sole to allow it to arch more easily, and if necessary I also cut the vamp lower. When the vamp is too high, I have trouble bending at the toe joints to rise onto half-pointe. When my shoes get dirty, I paint them a new color. At the end, each pair has had two or three coats of different colors.

When I was in France I adored wearing old ballet slippers all the time, and I never worried about it. I even used to dance without elastics, and with my strong feet, for the most part the shoes would stay on quite well. However, I once almost lost a shoe onstage, and finally I realized that I couldn't escape from the sewing of the elastics.

My ballet slippers are made in Paris by Repetto. I have a shoemaker there named Monsieur Serge who has always made my shoes, and he really is exceptional. The shoes I used to order years ago were much shorter and had a higher vamp than the ones I use now, since my foot has become larger and stronger. Because my feet change shape with time, every two years Monsieur Serge checks them.

I used to wear leather slippers, which are quite shiny. Now I wear canvas, so my tights and shoes seem to be made of the same material. I also like the way the canvas takes the shape of my foot. For girls it is different; I feel strongly about wanting to see the shiny pointe shoes on them. Those special shoes and feet should be seen by the audience.

I'm the only male dancer I know of who has had such an experience, but in Paris I wore pointe shoes for my beginning ballet classes. I was the only boy in the class, and the teacher didn't know how to instruct boys. She had the crazy idea to put me on pointe with the rest of the class. For six months I studied with her, and in a way the pointe work was beneficial—it strengthened my ankles and improved my high arches. Ironically, I was the best in the class!

I still sometimes do some pointe work to build up strength in my ankles. It will be good rehabilitation to reinforce the ligaments that I tore in a recent injury.

As I teach ballet to young boys, I notice that they really haven't any conception of how a ballet slipper should feel when it fits properly. Because the foot might look enormous and not very pleasing, the boys usually take a smaller size than they should. No matter—whether it feels tight or loose, the boys think it's normal. Sometimes I see that a boy absolutely cannot bend or stretch his toes to rise on half-pointe because his foot is cramped in the slippers. I am concerned, because not only does a scanty shoe impair movement, but it can eventually damage the foot.

Leslie Browne

It was a big thrill to put on my first pair of pointe shoes and to get up on pointe, but so far I've never had a pointe shoe that I've really liked. I keep adjusting and changing; in fact, I must have had at least ten different kinds of shoe orders in the past six years. As my strength, technique, placement, and, oddly enough, the shape of my foot all change, I need a different type of shoe. Now I'm wearing Freeds ordered with a medium winged vamp so that the top of the shoe covers my large bunion joint. I like a wide, square-shaped box but a very narrow, low-cut heel.

Since I wear Freeds, I don't have to do much to break them in. I pour alcohol around the tight areas to stretch them, and scrape off some of the leather sole to lighten them. Of course, I bang them to get rid of all the noise and make them as flexible as possible, and I brush Fabulon on them to lengthen their life. After I walk around a little and do some relevés, they're ready to go.

I'd much rather have someone else sew on my ribbons and elastics, but no one will do it, unless it's an extreme emergency. I try to sew enough shoes for a whole week in one sitting, but I always end up sewing them each night for the following day.

I wouldn't mind wearing ballet slippers like the men. They don't have to worry about foot problems resulting from pointe shoes, and it would be kind of fun. On the other hand, it would be harder to express my steps on half-pointe, because I wouldn't be all the way up on my toes and my movements would seem incomplete. On pointe I can pull and stretch away from the floor as far as possible.

It's essential to have the right kind of shoes at the right time. For certain ballets I will need a hard shoe, but generally I like them all fairly soft, except for the tip of the toe, which I always want to be hard. The rest of the shoe should be very supple so that I can use my foot fully. I don't want to feel an actual shoe on my foot; I want the shoe to become part of me.

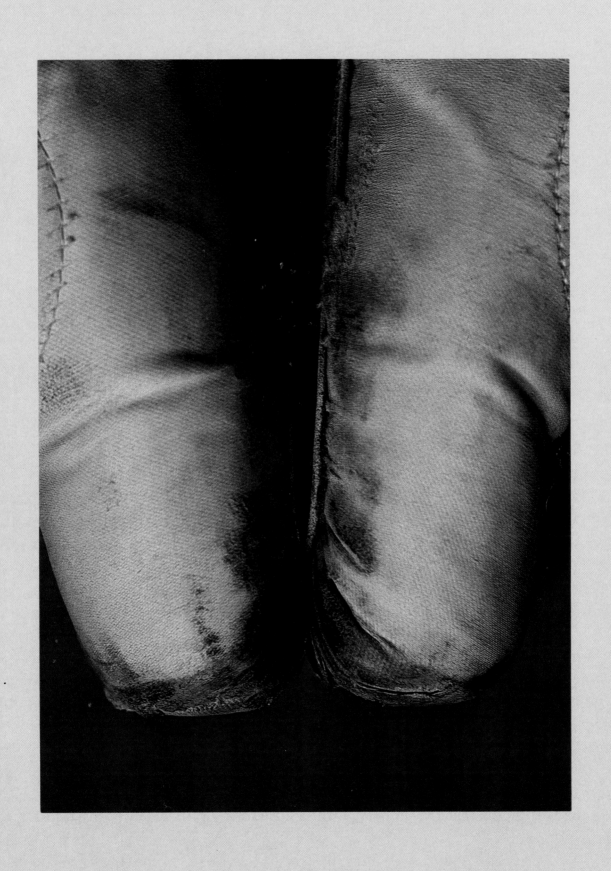

Fernando Bujones

It's as simple as this: good ballet slippers are ones I can dance in. I have leather slippers from Capezio that I give good performances in consistently. I have had bad slippers, too—ones that are either very soft or very slippery. After one performance and rehearsal, they break. Normally slippers last me quite a while. I can dance a full season of eight weeks with just two pairs. A pair can easily last me two or three months.

I crisscross my elastics, because the first time I performed a major role—it was *Konservatoriet* at the School of American Ballet Workshop Performance—I had sewn only one band across, and one of my shoes slipped off my heel. Luckily I was standing on half-pointe, and when I came down off it, I landed directly inside the shoe again. After that I said to myself, "No more—I'm not taking this risk," and I started crisscrossing two elastics on each shoe.

I don't glue my shoes to my tights for performances because the crisscrossed elastics are usually enough to keep the slippers on. If it's a pair that's beginning to get loose combined with tights that are slippery, I put a little rosin on the heels of my tights before putting my slippers on.

Depending a great deal on the sort of feet he has, sometimes ballet slippers can improve a dancer's line. In the end, however, what really counts is what your foot does in the slipper rather than what the slipper does on your foot.

Alexandra Radius

My pointe shoes are like my babies. I'm busy during my free time with them; in fact, I'm perpetually busy with my shoes. I like to work on adjusting my shoes by breaking them in cautiously and taking constant care of them. Since I can usually correct the faults of my pointe shoes, I don't throw them out if they aren't perfect. I bring them home and clean them and shellac them, I sew on ribbons and elastics, I do extra little repairs, and I put them on the radiator to dry the shellac thoroughly. Before I dance in the shoes to break them in, I put shellac inside the box and a little bit under the arch in order to have more control over where the shoe will break and bend; otherwise they bend in a way that I don't want. To keep the shape of the tip of the box and to take away some of the noise, I darn the tips. I hate noisy, clunky shoes. Since I don't have very tight-fitting shoes, I need to sew on a small loop of elastic to lace my ribbons through, and this helps hold the heel onto my foot. I also put glue on the heel, on the sides, and under the arch of my tights, which affixes the shoe to my foot. I love to break in my shoes smoothly during the slow and controlled pas de deux in the second act of *Swan Lake* or in *Adagio Hammer-klavier*. If I try to break them in by doing fouettés, the shoes will be ruined immediately.

For most performances I try to wear shoes that are well broken in, because if the shoes are too hard, I won't be able to feel the floor. Even though it's painful, I want to be aware of my toenails on the floor, because it forces me to pull up that much more to reduce the pressure on my toes. Only for the technically demanding roles like Odile are strong, hard shoes desirable.

I dance barefoot and I adore modern ballets, but I feel more natural in pointe shoes. Because I feel higher up, lighter, and more at ease, some steps are easier for me to do on pointe—like the pirouettes in attitude in *Giselle*. They're more difficult to do on half-pointe, because there's more of the foot to revolve on, which causes more resistance and slows the turns. Fouettés flow on pointe, and I can almost do them with my eyes closed.

Helgi Tomasson

A good pair of ballet shoes means that after I put them on, I can immediately go onstage and dance. Dancing is complicated enough without the trouble of breaking in ballet slippers. Even street shoes that are not supple are repugnant to me.

Now I wear canvas slippers by Gamba, which are good because they're so soft. I judge a pair of shoes by how they're cut and stitched. If the stitches that attach the sole to the canvas under the ball of the foot are jagged, it can throw off my balance. However, I rarely receive an inferior pair from Gamba, because the same craftsman consistently does my order.

I want the sole to conform to my arch when I point my foot, so I order snug and flexible slippers. Because of this fit, I am almost as sensitive to the floor in my slippers as I am in bare feet. Quite often the stage is not flawless; even on linoleum the cracks in the wooden floor underneath can be dangerous, especially during a turning combination. It's an advantage to be able to feel the problem spots so that you can avoid them. However, I need the protection of slippers for classical ballet variations in which there are multiple turns and jumps.

It's possible to borrow tights, costumes, or make-up, but never ballet slippers. My slippers must fit and belong to my own feet. In fact, when I travel I never pack my shoes into the suitcase that will be stored in the baggage compartment; I always carry them on the plane with me for safety. Wearing another dancer's shoes would be a disaster —probably more psychologically than physically. During one of my first performances with the New York City Ballet, however, one of my slippers split down the middle. I had just gone onstage, and I couldn't dance with this shoe. Fortunately, a dancer who had been watching from the wings gave me one of his shoes. Although his shoe was nearly identical to mine, it was molded to his foot's shape. But since everything happened in an instant and I was so relieved and grateful, I couldn't think ill of the shoe.

Lately my wife has been sewing the elastics onto my slippers; I used to do it. It's extremely important that they be sewn over the insteps with precision. Even the most minute variation in the placement can cause the shoe to slip off the heel or at least to feel loose. When I am onstage and the elastic doesn't hit me on the regular spot over my instep, my mind keeps going down to my foot, and it shouldn't. Nothing should distract me when I am onstage dancing.

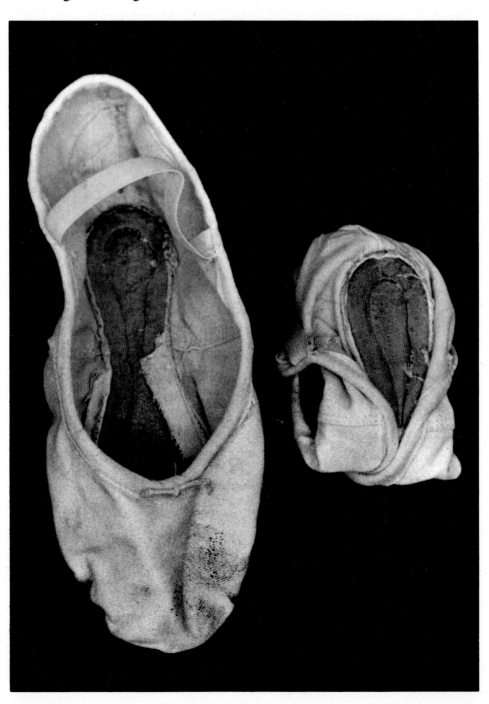

Karin von Aroldingen

When I began dancing on pointe at the age of twelve, I was in tears just from having the shoes on for five minutes. But my teacher told me, "You will never become a classical dancer unless you dance on pointe," and I'll never forget those words. Since I'd inherited my mother's bunion problem, she was sympathetic, and like a good mother, she always massaged my sore feet and sewed the ribbons on my pointe shoes for me.

Now I'm at ease with pointe work. Very often Balanchine's choreography is so intricate and fast that a heavy shoe just wouldn't be suitable. I worked hard to toughen and strengthen my feet to be able to dance in his demanding ballets. I still have aching toes. Nevertheless, I cannot imagine not dancing on pointe, and for me dancing on half-pointe or barefoot is more disagreeable.

I wear Freed shoes because of their lightness and their unique orangey-pink satin, which appeals to Mr. Balanchine. Shiny pointe shoes have a lovely delicate look, so I don't dull my shoes with powder or rosin. I know dancers who turn their ribbons inside out to the matte side, but I like it all shiny—shiny satin shoes and shiny satin ribbons.

By a process of trial and error, I have figured out how to handle my pointe shoes. Once I took a shoe apart and examined its insides. With a few materials—glue, nails, satin—a pointe shoe is constructed. Basically, a hard tip and a flexible shank are all that I really bother about: I have a standard-size vamp and width, and I don't sew elastics into my ribbons or use glue on my heels, because rosin keeps the heels on efficiently. I break the shoes in by bending and cracking the soles and then tearing the backs of the shanks out. As a result, I can feel the floor and use my feet to grasp it. Because they're handmade, every shoe is different; every pair can't be fabulous, and I've learned to cope with shoes that may not be perfect. For certain ballets Mr. Balanchine advises his ballerinas that hard, new shoes aren't needed and that we should pay attention to the noise of our pointe shoes, especially in a ballet like *Serenade* with all its pas de bourrées and running steps. Before a performance it's very noisy backstage, because so many pointe shoes are being banged on the floor to diminish their noise and hardness.

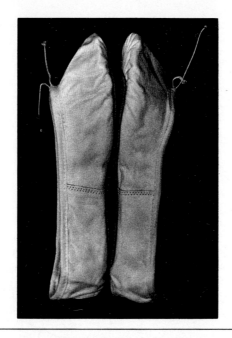

Kenneth McCombie

Ballet slippers are indispensable, and like anything else that's important to me, I give them my time, energy, and thought. Honestly, without my slippers I couldn't dance as well. My feet are not tough and I need the protection of ballet slippers, except for the rare ballet or modern dance that is especially choreographed for bare feet.

Originally I was studying ballroom dancing, but after seeing Rudolf Nureyev perform, I was inspired to become a ballet dancer. But living in a small village in Scotland and being a bit frightened of the talk, my mother didn't encourage me at all to study ballet. It was my idependent decision to become a ballet dancer. I welcome sweat and ballets that challenge my technique and stamina; in fact, these are my favorite kinds of ballets—ones like *Romeo and Juliet* and the "Polovtsian Dances" from *Prince Igor*. Only when I feel completely drained, mentally and physically, do I feel I've given a good performance. I want to work vigorously to be able to achieve the best, and I'm obliged to make sure that all the ingredients of the dance, including my shoes, are in working order.

I need to feel confident when I dance. That's one of the reasons why I sew elastics onto my slippers. I know the exact way in which they should be sewn and how tight I need them. Also, I must have shoes that hug my feet and feel secure.

My shoes are from Gamba in London. I order a regular British size 8 slipper cut lower to measure four inches from the front and three inches from the back. (The four inches are measured from the end of the sole by the pleating to the drawstring knot on top; the three inches are measured from the end of the sole under the heel to the top of the heel by the Achilles' tendon.) This gives my shoes a nice round shape.

I've been rather lucky with these shoes. Because they have a lovely soft sole and the leather gives so easily they break in within five minutes. Unless it's an emergency, I never go straight onstage with completely new shoes; I always warm-up in them first.

Gelsey Kirkland

Once I was called out from class and told to hurry on over to the State Theatre to replace Patricia McBride as the Sugar Plum Fairy in *Nutcracker*; she had injured herself and it was an emergency. In all my life I had never done a performance under those conditions. Not only did I wear her costume, but I had to dance in her pointe shoes; I had only ten minutes to prepare, and I didn't have any shoes of my own that were already sewn. I just threw on her shoes, and even though they didn't look exactly right on my feet, I actually enjoyed dancing in them. It was amazing how differently I danced and felt in another dancer's shoes. When I went on pointe in Patty's shoes, I felt as if I could have balanced forever; it was an effort *not* to hold a balance!

Over the years my pointe shoes have become a little bit shorter and wider. When I first joined the New York City Ballet, I wanted my foot to look long and narrow, even though I have a very wide foot. I also wanted the shoes to look tight, so I squeezed my foot into shoes that were much too narrow, which was terribly constricting for my tendons. It looks very nice to have a tapered toe, but these days I am accepting nature and choosing comfort over vanity.

Depending on the quality of the shipment I receive, some shoes will collapse immediately, while others will last for ten performances. Because some shoes have lumpy, distorted tips, heels that are too long, or shanks that aren't equal in length, I have to treat each shoe individually. If the vamp is not long enough, I have to sew on an extra piece of elastic across the instep near the toes; sometimes I have to stretch a shoe out more or not at all. It varies tremendously.

Before I even put on a new pair of pointe shoes, I put a few layers of Fabulon on the box and the shank to keep the shoe strong a bit longer. To prevent slipping, I scale the sole with a special scraper that is available only in Europe. I also shave the shank with a razor blade; otherwise, it's too thick. What I do then depends on the ballet. If I must be very quiet, I dab a little alcohol right underneath the pleating and hammer it until that part of the shoe is soft. Hammering is really exhausting and time-consuming. If I must have extremely strong shoes for a ballet like *Theme and Variations*, I simply put my shoes on and hit the floor several times. However, my main concern is that I not make any noise. I would rather that the shoe be a little bit too soft than be noisy.

I always mold my pointe shoes to my feet. Early in the day of a performance, I wrap paper towels around my toes and stuff my feet into new pointe shoes. With the help of the alcohol that I pour on my shoes, they stretch to a comfortable size. Even if I don't rehearse or take class in them, I at least walk around in them. As the shoes finish drying, I stick an old shoe inside each one of them to maintain the shoe's new contours.

I am waiting for the day when I will have magical pointe shoes and there will be a gigantic magnet under the floor of the stage; it will attract the shoes and have the power to pull me around. For example, when I step onto pointe to balance during the Rose Adagio from *The Sleeping Beauty*, this magnet would brace my foot to keep me on my toes for an extraordinarily effortless balance...

Peter Martins

I prefer canvas ballet slippers to leather for several reasons. Even though the canvas is soft, the slippers don't overstretch, whereas leather ones really spread out of shape. And canvas slippers are so easy to break in. After a few warm-ups at the barre, they fit. I also like the matte finish of the canvas, as I've always felt that shiny leather disrupts the line of the leg. However, in certain ballets this shiny look is required, and leather slippers are essential.

I have a man in Paris who makes my slippers. They were designed to allow my feet complete mobility and sensitivity. First, he took an impression of my feet, and we both decided how the shoes should be constructed for my needs. It's absolutely necessary to feel the floor through the slippers; they should be like gloves.

My ballet slippers are definitely the most important article of all my ballet equipment. I couldn't dance—I'd be lost—without them. Like most dancers, I feel I can dance better if my footwear is in order. However, I would never put the blame on my shoes if I danced poorly. In an emergency I'm sure I could go out onstage and dance just as well in another dancer's shoes—unless they belonged to someone Villella-sized. Then it would be impossible.

I don't clean my ballet slippers, but I do spray them whatever color they need to be for each ballet. Luckily I have a wonderful friend at the New York City Ballet who expertly sews my elastics on my shoes. Usually dancers take care of their own shoes, but I trust this person to follow my exact instructions.

I was fascinated when I saw the male folk dancers who dance on pointe in Russia. Having tried to stand on pointe myself, I fully appreciate how difficult and painful it is. As a choreographer, I am finding that the creative possibilities for dancers on pointe are far greater than on half-pointe. Although there are fantastic things that one can choreograph for men, I find it more of a challenge to choreograph for women, because pointe work adds an entirely different dimension to explore.

Ann Marie De Angelo

Dancing on pointe is a major part of my life—it is a necessity—and the pointe shoe is the major problem of my career. I can have shoes that are the same size, but if they aren't flexible or if the pleats are sloppy, I won't be able to turn or relevé in them. Like most ballerinas, I go through tremendous heartache because of my shoes; I know I can't dance when my feet don't feel right. I have hundreds of pointe shoes in my dressing room, but I can honestly say that I have none that really feel decent; only some that I can pretend to rehearse in or perform in. For years I've been experimenting with shoes to try to find ones that fit exactly. I'm still looking.

Only after I break in my shoes can I decide whether they will be comfortable and how much strength or support they have. When I have to do thirty-two fouettés, I need a strong shoe, whereas for jumps I need a soft, pliable shank—a rather worn pair. My breaking-in procedure begins by cutting the satin off the tip of the shoe and removing half the shank for increased flexibility of the arch. When I put the shoes on, I pour a little alcohol or water on the box to soften it. Finally, I do a few warm-up barre exercises or a rehearsal in them. I do a lot of bravura roles, probably because I'm so muscular and have a strong technique. Especially for these types of roles I need to put glue and rosin on the bottoms of my tights to keep my shoes securely on my feet.

I can wear a good pair of shoes endlessly. I had a perfect pair of shoes that endured two tours of dancing *Viva Vivaldi!*, four weeks of repertory, and two performances of *Don Quixote*. By reconstructing the shoe with Fabulon, shellac, and glue, I preserved the vamp and the box and wore them till they no longer felt like pointe shoes.

When Gerald Arpino was choreographing *L'Air d'Esprit*, he took a few of us to visit Olga Spessivtzeva for additional coaching and advice. I brought a pair of my pointe shoes, and she said, "Too heavy, too heavy." The ones she wore in her day were so light. Today shoes are constructed with thick materials and nails, which causes the shoes to be quite bulky. I think it's harder to jump and work the feet now because of this.

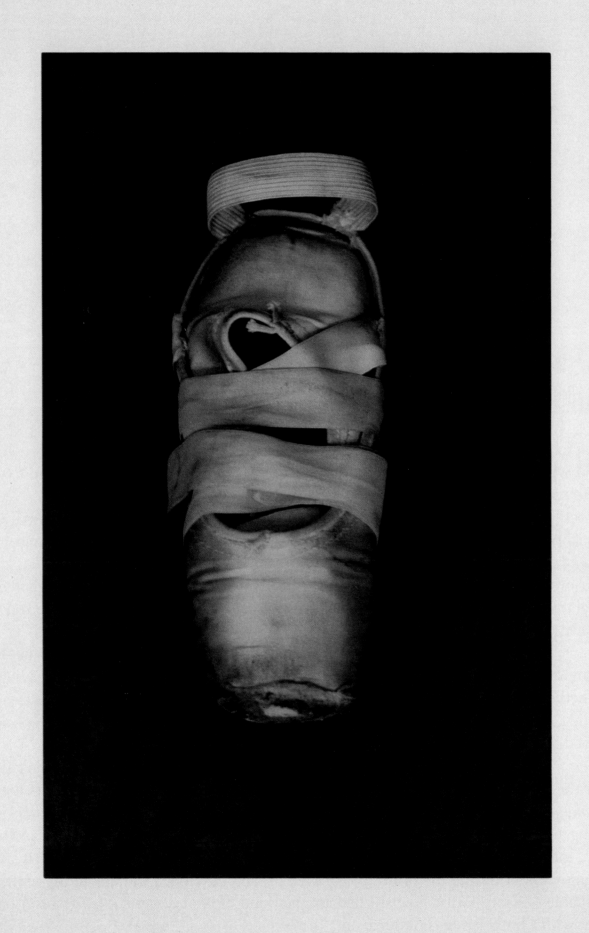

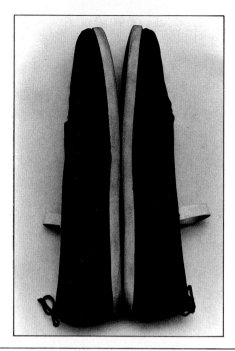

Gary Chryst

I don't think people are born to wear shoes, and somehow, they never feel natural to me. I enjoy dancing in bare feet; it's a wonderful sensation actually to touch the ground while I'm dancing. But then I don't have my shoes to protect my feet and to give me a better line.

When I first began to study ballet, I wore Selva leather slippers. Now I wear a special order of canvas Capezio slippers in a size 11½—the same size as Christian Holder, but he's six feet four and I'm only five feet seven. My feet are very large and flat; I also have a protruding heel, so the heel of my slipper must be made a half inch higher than normal to accommodate this. Because the cotton drawstrings cut into my feet like ropes, I order elastic.

I'm basically more of a character dancer, so although I do dance in ballet slippers, most of the time I dance in other kinds of shoes. It doesn't make much difference to me whether I break in my slippers or not. I'm used to them; I use them for class every day and they don't bother me. It's different with my character shoes, which are specially designed for each role. I have to figure out each pair to find out how it works.

Dancing in a heel is a lot harder, and generally character shoes don't bend under the metatarsals. In my opinion, when Oscar Araiz ordered authentic boots for me in *Romeo and Juliet*, he was thinking more of the audience than of the dancer who was wearing them. I knew he wanted me to project a certain image, so I worked in those heavy, inflexible boots. As a result, my arches became so cramped, particularly from jumping without having the full use of my feet, that I developed bursitis in my arch and was unable to dance for two days. I had another kind of boot designed, using a soft ballet slipper with a leather extension sewn on.

The black velvet Chinese shoes I wear for *Parade* are perhaps the finest shoes that Capezio has ever made for me. So far, they've lasted six years. They're a little difficult to wear, because I can't bend or stretch my feet in them. However, the soles are springy and the choreography is fairly bouncy and calls for the feet to be in a flexed position much of the time. The moment I saw the photograph of Léonide Massine dancing *Parade* in 1917, I was impressed. In the Picasso costume and the elaborate Chinese make-up, he looked magnificent. So for appearance, I'm willing to sacrifice a little bit of comfort.

When Ashton's ballet *The Dream* was first being set on The Joffrey Ballet, I was rehearsing the role of Bottom, which is a very complex acting and dancing role and one of the few male roles that call for pointe work. Unfortunately, my feet are not flexible, and it was an incredible strain on my body simply to push my toes forward in the pointe shoes in order to stand directly on the tips of my toes. I did look very funny, though, pounding my toes into the floor like a donkey. At the first run-through I did my variation very well—I even held a long balance—but the strain on my body was too great. My back dislocated, and I was out for a week. Since then, I am sympathetic to girls who dance on pointe—it's torture.

Galina Panov

I actually have a need to dance on pointe. When I'm sitting at dinner, I have such an urge to stand on my toes that I find myself doing exercises underneath the table. I even feel more comfortable in pointe shoes than in street shoes. As with any new shoes, it's difficult when they're new, and it's hard work to break them in. I do this by doing the barre during class with new shoes or by doing some relevé combinations at the end of class. I usually like older shoes, because they're stretched out enough and are no longer noisy. But in something like the Rose Adagio from *The Sleeping Beauty*, it's important for the legs and feet to look very pretty, so for this part I wear shoes that are practically new. In some ballets I use Capezios for certain variations and perhaps Freeds for others. For bravura ballets like *Don Quixote*, I need very strong shoes that can stay hard for a long time; I find Capezios to be best for this sort of role.

From many years of standing on pointe, my toes have become squared-off, which is good for dancing on pointe. I was twelve years old when I started pointe work; it's not wise to begin at six or seven as some children do. All the exercises must first be practiced on half-pointe until the legs and back are strong enough. Pointe work is not at all easy, but it's fun because it's so romantic. That's one reason why so many little girls dream of pointe shoes and dancing on pointe.

In order to come onstage and be able to dance on pointe without strain, it's essential to work very hard on pointe technique in the classroom. Especially in America, where there is so much competition, pointe work is wonderfully strong because everyone concentrates so much on technique. When I was in Russia I worked on my technique in school, but in the theater I didn't think too much about it. In America and Europe the dancer never stops working on technique, even after leaving school, and now I do too.

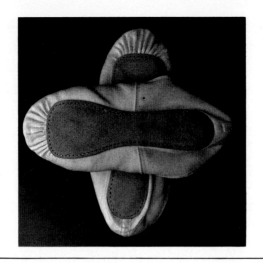

Sean Lavery

Even though Mr. Balanchine doesn't want the men in the New York City Ballet to use canvas slippers, because they really look shabby when they get dirty, I use them. I'm extra careful about keeping my slippers clean and white with white shoe polish, though, and that's why Mr. Balanchine doesn't seem to object. Leather slippers are horrible for me; when they stretch out, I look as if I'm wearing socks. They just can't keep their form. I wear Capezio canvas ballet slippers in size 10½EE.

The ballet slippers that are comfortable for me have low vamps, elastic drawstrings, and the ability to stretch sufficiently while still holding a nice shape. I recently began ordering my slippers with lower-cut vamps and heels because they're more comfortable and make my feet look better. Although I used to have cotton drawstrings, I prefer the give of the elastic ones. As a safety precaution to hold my shoes to my feet I always rub rosin on the heels of my tights and sew one elastic band across each instep.

I hate breaking in new shoes and sewing on elastics, so I do both of these chores as quickly as I can. If my shoes are good, I can simply walk onstage with a brand-new pair; but more often than not I get shoes that cramp my toes. As it is essential that my toes be able to spread in order to be aware of the surface and free to move, the slippers have to be softened a bit and my feet must become accustomed to them. I can usually break them in during one class.

When my feet are swollen, any new shoes, good or bad, will make them ache. Sometimes ballet slippers can cause pain due to the bulky knots of the drawstrings. When I kneel, slide, or do a double tour en l'air to the knee, the knot will occasionally press into a nerve in my foot. I have had sores that lasted an entire week from that.

In Germany I was wearing the most unbelievably uncomfortable ballet slippers. They were so tight and they seemed never to conform to my feet. Since my toes were being squeezed, I could hardly bend them to do a relevé. Whenever I pointed my foot, the sole would buckle. They were so stiff and hard that all the male dancers would have to crack them in doors. These shoes were also the ugliest in the world! Like many of the dancers in the Frankfurt Opera Ballet, I wanted to order another brand of shoes, but the administration didn't like that idea. We were allotted only six pairs of shoes a year, which were supposed to last us for all classes, rehearsals, and ballet and opera performances. If we asked for more than that, we needed to have special permission forms signed by the director of the costume shop. My first year I needed eight additional pairs of slippers; still, I had to preserve each pair by repairing their ever-widening holes.

Now, as a principal dancer in the New York City Ballet, I use about thirty pairs a year. I don't have a restriction on shoes, but I wouldn't abuse this privilege. I think that a lot of girls put on pointe shoes, say they're disgusting, and throw them out. If my shoes are unacceptable, I either return them to the person who handles our shoes or use them for class or rehearsal; I won't throw them away. In fact, as long as my shoes fit properly, I don't mind their being old, and some pairs I wear for several seasons. I clean them, and if they are well constructed, they will last. In Saratoga I sewed and dyed a pair of slippers for *Kammermusik No. 2* and wore them for three performances there, two performances in Copenhagen, and two performances in New York; however, I wore them only for that particular ballet. All in all, I'm not terribly affected by my shoes, but I always feel better when I know my feet look right and I'm able to use my toes.

Marianna Tcherkassky

Although dancing on pointe is sometimes painful, it's one of the most gratifying ways for me to express myself. When I first joined American Ballet Theatre in the corps de ballet, I was wearing Capezios, and I didn't pay much attention to my shoes. When I was given additional responsibilities, I became more aware of my body and what I was doing. I also realized that my pointe shoes were not really giving me the kind of support I needed. I finally settled on a pointe shoe that gives me the right kind of support and is very comfortable. But not every dancer can wear these strong Austrian shoes made by Schachtner; they take a lot of getting used to. Compared with Capezios, Schachtners have a much flatter tip. They also seem to stretch out a little bit too much as I work in them, and I must keep wrapping tissues around my toes to keep the shoes snug. But because of the flatter tip I can balance better, and I also feel much more pulled up in them.

I step on the box and the sole to make them a bit more flexible, and I do a few relevés or perhaps a rehearsal in them; that's all the breaking-in my shoes need. Actually, I hate breaking in new shoes. I get very attached to my shoes, so I keep them as long as I can. I sometimes wear one pair of pointe shoes for a whole week of rehearsals. If my shoes are good enough, I can wear them for a couple of performances and then for rehearsals. Actually, my mother is the one who really gets attached to my shoes—she treasures them. She's saving the shoes I wore for my first *Giselle* and my first *Nutcracker*.

Sewing the elastics and ribbons on my shoes is tedious. Usually I take six pairs, sit in the living room and sew all night. Recently I started sewing elastics into the ribbons, which allows the ribbons to give and adjust to my movements; I had been having trouble with my calves, which were getting cramped from tight ribbons. This takes even more time, but it's worth it.

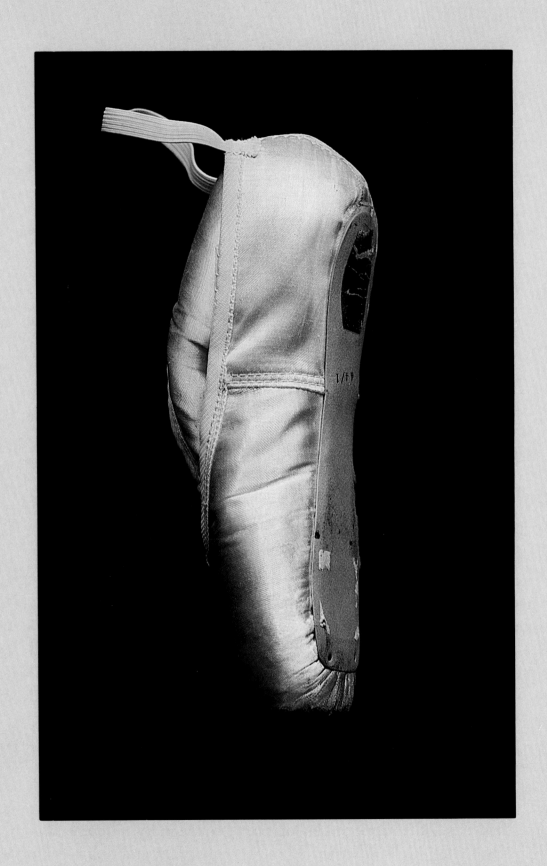

Burton Taylor

I wear Gamba shoes, which are made in England. They're patterned after the Russian ballet slippers—cut down in the vamp, in the heel, and on the sides by certain measurements. They also have a very narrow sole. Because of their light canvas and thin sole, my shoes don't give much support, but they conform to my feet very well. I just have to be extra careful to resist the floor when I land from a jump, or my feet will take too much of a beating.

Ballet slippers are constructed to conform to the foot, and if they fit well, they will not do anything to hinder the extension of the line of the leg. Slippers that fit well continue the proper elongation and flow of energy.

Some pairs of slippers are better than others, even when they're all cut to the same specified measurements. Sometimes they just look a certain way because the toe area curves out, which helps the pointed foot form a good line. Those shoes I consider special, and they automatically feel wonderful.

During one of my tours as a guest artist in Italy with Carla Fracci, we rehearsed in a studio that had a very old wooden floor that was rutted, ridged, and splinted. Because I was destroying a pair of shoes every day I rehearsed, and I didn't have that many pairs with me, one of the dancers gave me his shoes. That was the only time I ever wore another dancer's ballet slippers. Having been broken in by different feet, the shape of the slippers was completely different. They were too tight and didn't conform to my arch; in fact, the sole was stiff and flat. A photographer was there that day taking pictures, and in the photographs my feet hardly resemble my own.

Patricia McBride

I think I'm one of the few dancers who prefers really soft pointe shoes. My Freeds are specially ordered to be very light, with a pliable shank called a Phillips insole. I also bang each shoe twenty times on the floor to make it quiet onstage.

If I dance in big, heavy shoes, I will defeat my purpose, which is trying to appear light. I need my shoes to be soft especially just underneath my toes, where the shoes are pleated, in order to feel and grip the floor and to feel free and be able to dance with abandon. I like to cover space and travel through various movements as I dance.

Every dancer has her own way of standing on her toes. My toes are straight, but I have a high arch; therefore, I bend the shank to break it in and to have the sole of the shoe close to my arch. Although a lot of people criticize my way of standing "over" my feet instead of pulling back on the insteps with a straight arch, I feel I look best this way and it's the most comfortable for the structure of my feet. I have the strength and control to stand like this, but it might be wrong for somebody else.

Sewing on our own ribbons and elastics is part of the dancer's tradition and a task that we do every day. It is also a sort of superstition—if we don't sew them on ourselves, we won't have a good performance or something will go wrong.

I never throw my pointe shoes away after a performance. The cost of a pair of pointe shoes is astronomical, so I use them either for another performance or for class. It's unbelievable how many pairs of shoes a week we go through in the company. Also, pointe shoes are made by hand. They've been handmade for all these years, and they are one of the few things that haven't been taken over by the machine. This is another reason why I try to wear my shoes for as long as possible.

Graphic Credits

The text of this book was set in a film version of Janson that
has been redrawn from the face created by Nicholas Kis. Hungarian born,
he traveled to Holland in the late seventeenth century and most probably learned the
trade from the master type founder Dirk Voskens. At the time of Janson's creation it was unsurpassed
for character, with its thicks and thins giving it a certain clarity and grace.
Having redrawn Janson several times for Stempel, Herman Zapf eventually created a face known as
Zapf International, which is the display face in this book. Although it bears resemblance
to the older face, its italic has a quality of having been drawn with
a brush rather than engraved. Both are available from I.T.C., a new
collection of type faces created specifically for the Mergenthaler V.I.P. system.

This book was photo-composed in film on the V.I.P. by TypoGraphics Communications, Inc., New York, N.Y.
The black-and-white reproductions were scanned by Alithochrome Corporation, Hauppauge, N.Y.
The color separations were produced by Offset-Separations, New York, N.Y., and Turin, Italy.
The book was printed by Rae Publishing Co., Inc., Cedar Grove, N.J., and
bound by Sendor Bindery, New York, N.Y.

Production and manufacturing were directed by Ellen McNeilly.
Design and graphics were directed by R. D. Scudellari.
Graphics were styled by Sara Eisenman.